Total Restoration

A closer look at the Restoration of GOD in the Christian's life; proof that GOD restores.

Evangelist Thomas Couch

The Spotted Feather

I would like to dedicate this book to the readers. I would also like to dedicate it to my Precious Mother and all of my family. And with all due gratitude, I would like to dedicate it to every person that is involved in the ministries worldwide. For their hard work, dedication, and love and kindness to all of those who sought the LORD, and found HIM as a result of the many great ministries out there.

May GOD bless you all beyond measure.

Sincerely in Christ,

Evangelist Thomas Couch

REVIVE-ALL MINISTRIES

ISAIAH 57:15

* All Scripture is given from The King James Version of The Bible.

Introduction

My dear Christian friend, it is my hope, prayer, and whole heart's desire that this book, "Total Restoration," will be a blessing to every reader.

I pray that it will open your eyes to the fact that GOD wants to restore you in every area of your life.

I pray that it will also open your eyes to some of the tricks that Satan and his unclean army will bring against you, in efforts to destroy every area of your life.

And I pray that it will help you to overcome Satan and his unclean army, and step into the total restoration that GOD is offering you.

I pray that it will help you to live the abundant, victorious life that Jesus wants you to live, and enjoy the Bible's full rewards.

Hope you enjoy reading, "Total Restoration."

Evangelist Thomas Couch

* All Scripture is given from The King James Version of The Bible.

Contents

Chapter One

Total Restoration

22.) And he shall send Jesus Christ, which before was preached unto you:

23.) Whom the heaven must receive until the times of restitution of all things, which God hath spoken by the mouth of all his holy Prophets since the world began.

ACTS 3:20-21

My dear Christian friend, this verse mentions the times of restitution of all things. I will define restitution of all things very briefly. It means "Total Restoration."

The time for total restoration is now. GOD wants to restore you in every area of your life. This verse says that GOD has spoken of total restoration since the world began, and the time for it is now.

The Word of GOD says that Satan came to steal, kill and destroy every area of your life. But Jesus came to give you an abundant, victorious life. Jesus came to give you total restoration in every area of your life, and that means now is the time for total restoration. Total restoration is available for you here and now. Let's look at a verse to prove this.

The thief cometh not, but for to steal, and to kill, and to destroy: I am come that they might have life, and that they might have it more abundantly.

JOHN 10:10

So, you see, Jesus came to give us an abundant, victorious life in every area of our lives. That, my friend, is total restoration.

When you were living a sinful life and Satan was taking everything from you, GOD was storing it up to restore it to you, when you become just and start living for HIM. Let's look at a verse to prove this.

A good man leaveth an inheritance to his Children's Children: and the wealth of the sinner is laid up for the just.

PROVERBS 13:22

So, you see, it says the wealth of the sinner is laid up for the just. Everything that Satan took from you when you were living sinful, GOD has stored it up for you when you become just and start living for HIM. GOD wants to give you total restoration in every area of your life.

If you have hate and prejudice in your life, GOD wants to take that and restore it with love. If you have sadness, GOD wants to take that and restore it with joy and happiness. If you are living a life of defeat, GOD wants to take that and restore it with victory in every area of your life. That is what total restoration is about. And the time for total restoration is now.

You have to make a choice to accept total restoration. The Word of GOD contains everything you need for total restoration. Some people just will not accept the Word of GOD. You can give them a verse saying that they can have peace, and they will give you a verse claiming tribulation in their lives. You can give some people a verse saying that they can have prosperity, and they will give you a verse claiming poverty for their lives. I don't know about you, but I want the peace and prosperity for my life. It is a choice that you have to make for yourself, to accept the Word of GOD for your life.

My dear Christian friend, the Word of GOD is yours right now. You are who it says you are. You can have what it says you can have. You can do what it says you can do. That is what total restoration is about. Total restoration is about accepting what the Word of GOD has for you, and applying it to your life.

When you make a choice to accept the Word of GOD for your life, and start applying it to your life, you will have good success in every area of your life. Let's look at a verse to prove this.

This book of the law shall not depart out of thy mouth; but thou shalt meditate therein day and night, that thou mayest observe to do according to all that is written therein: for then thou shalt make thy way Prosperous, and then thou shalt have good success.

JOSHUA 1:8

So, you see, when you observe to do according to all that is written in the Word of GOD, then you will make your way prosperous, and have good success in every area of your life. When you accept what the Word of GOD says about your life, and start applying the Word of GOD to your life, you will be prosperous in every area of your life, and you will have good success in every area of your life. That is what total restoration is about, and the time for total restoration is now.

The Word of GOD is perfect for changing your life, in every area of your life. Let's look at a verse to prove this.

The law of the Lord is perfect, Converting the soul: the testimony of the Lord is sure, making wise the simple.

PSALMS 19:7

So, you see, the Word of GOD is perfect in Converting your life. The Word of GOD is sure in changing your life. The Word of GOD is sure to bring total restoration in every area of your life. The Word of GOD is indeed perfect to bring total restoration in every area of your life.

It is up to you to make the choice to accept the Word of GOD for your life and to start applying it to your life. When you do, then it will without a doubt bring total restoration into your life.

GOD says in HIS Word, that he sets before you, life and death, blessings and cursing. But the choice is yours to choose life or death, blessings or cursing. Just like I said, it is a choice that you have to make for yourself. Let's look at a verse to prove this.

I call heaven and earth to record this day against you, that I have set before you, life and death, blessings and cursing: therefore, choose life, that both thou and thy seed may live.

DEUTERONOMY 30:19

Remember, I said that some people will not accept the Word of GOD for their lives. Some people will choose death instead of life. Some people will choose cursing instead of blessings. The Word of GOD is abundant life in every area of your life, and the Word of GOD is abundant blessings in every area of your life. That, my dear Christian friend, is what total restoration is about, and the time for total restoration in your life is now.

It is time for us Christians to accept the Word of GOD in our lives for what GOD intended it for. That is total restoration in every area of our lives.

GOD gave us the Word of GOD for total restoration in every area of our lives. GOD gave us the Word of GOD, and it will accomplish total restoration in every area of our lives when we accept it and start applying it to our lives. Let's look at a verse to prove this.

So shall my word be that goeth forth out of my mouth: it shall not return unto me void, but it shall accomplish that which I please, and it shall prosper in the thing whereto I sent it. ISAIAH 55:11

This verse is saying that the Word of GOD will accomplish what pleases GOD, and that the Word of GOD will prosper in the thing that HE sent it to do. GOD has sent us HIS Word for total restoration in every area of our lives.

GOD wants you to have total restoration in every area of your life, but the choice is yours. I say to you today, choose total restoration for your life. Accept the Word of GOD for your life, and start applying it to your life, in every area of your life today. Choose life and blessings, choose the Word of GOD, and choose total restoration.

Then you will be able to live that abundant, victorious life that Jesus wants you to live, and enjoy the Bible's full rewards.

That, my friend, is "Total Restoration."

Hallelujah!

Chapter Two

Total Restoration in Love

22.) But the fruit of the Spirit is love, joy, peace, longsuffering, gentleness, goodness, faith,

23.) Meekness, temperance: against such there is no law.

GALATIANS 5:22-23

Praise GOD! My friend, GOD wants to give you total restoration in love. You may have learned how to hate people, or you may be prejudiced towards others, or you may have become unforgiving in your life. Those are the things of Satan, but GOD wants to show you how to love at all times, just like HE does. GOD wants to give you total restoration in love.

When you start living for GOD, the Holy Spirit comes and dwells inside of you. In our opening verse, it says that the fruit of the Spirit is love. That is the way the Holy Spirit behaves, so if HE is inside of you, then you should have love for others, just the way HE does.

The only thing GOD hates is evil and sin. HE loves the sinner, but hates the sin. The Word of GOD tells us to hate evil, but it does not tell us to hate the person doing it. Let's look at a verse to prove this.

Ye that love the Lord, hate evil: he Preserveth the souls of his Saints; he delivereth them out of the hand of the wicked.

PSALMS 97:10

So, you see, the Word of GOD tells us to hate evil, not the person doing it. When GOD gives you total restoration in love, then you will love the person but hate the evil. That is what total restoration is all about, and now is the time for total restoration in love.

If you cannot love at all times the way GOD does, then how are you going to be able to tell others about GOD and HIS goodness, so they can get total restoration in every area of their lives the way GOD wants to give it to them?

The Word of GOD says a friend loves at all times. GOD is our friend that loves at all times, and HE wants to teach us to love at all times. Let's look at a verse to prove this.

A friend loveth at all times, and a brother is born for adversity.

PROVERBS 17:17

So, you see, GOD wants to give us total restoration in love so that we can love people at all times, just the way that HE loves them at all times. That my friend, is what total restoration in love is all about, and now is the time for total restoration in our lives.

My dear Christian friend, everybody wants to be loved. Jesus Christ gives us the best example of how we should love others in the Word of GOD. Jesus loves everybody in the world so much, that HE gave HIS precious life for them, so that they could be saved and enjoy total restoration in their lives. Let's look at a verse to prove this.

12.) This is my Commandment, That ye love one another, as I have loved you.

13.) Greater love hath no man than this, that a man lay down his life for his friends.

JOHN 15:12-13

Praise GOD! My dear Christian friend, when you start allowing the love of the Holy Spirit to start flowing through you, then you can actually love people enough to lay down your very life for them. Jesus said in this verse for us to love people as HE has loved us. HE laid down HIS life for us, that is how much HE loved us. That my friend, is what total restoration in love is all about, and now is the time for total restoration.

The way to learn to love the way GOD wants us to, is by keeping the Word of GOD. We have to study the Word of GOD, and allow GOD to give us total restoration in love, so that love can be perfected in our lives. Let's look at a verse to prove this.

But whoso keepeth his word, in him verily is the love of God perfected: hereby know that we are in him.

1st JOHN 2:5

So, you see, it is by keeping the Word of GOD, that GOD perfects HIS love in us. GOD wants to perfect HIS love in us. That, my friend, is what total restoration in love is all about, and now is the time for total restoration in our lives.

Do not hold on to hate, bitterness, or unforgiveness in your life, it will hinder your relationship with GOD, and with other people. Let's look at a verse to prove this.

14.) For if ye forgive men their trespasses, your heavenly Father will also forgive you:

15.) But if ye forgive not men their trespasses, neither will your Father forgive your trespasses.

JOHN 6:14-15

So, you see, if you have unforgiveness in your life and do not forgive others, then GOD will not forgive you. If you allow GOD to give you total restoration in love the way that HE wants to, it will help you to get rid of unforgiveness and forgive others and love them the same way that HE loves them. That my friend, is what total restoration in love is all about, and now is the time for you to allow GOD to give you total restoration in every area of your life.

GOD wants to make HIS love in you perfect, and that is total restoration in love. When you come to know GOD, the first thing HE wants to restore in you is love. Love is the very first thing mentioned in the Fruit of the Spirit. And GOD wants us to be rooted and grounded in love. Let's look at a verse to prove this.

That Christ may dwell in your hearts by faith; that ye being rooted and grounded in love.

EPHESIANS 3:17

So, you see, GOD wants us to be rooted and grounded in love, so that we can love at all times. GOD wants to make HIS love in you perfect and give you total restoration in love.

My dear Christian friend, Satan will do his best to keep you from getting total restoration in love. That is because love never fails. Let's look at a verse to prove this.

Charity never faileth: but whether there be Prophecies, they shall fail; whether there be tongues, they shall cease; whether there be knowledge, it shall vanish away.

1st CORINTHIANS 13:8

That first word Charity, actually means love. This verse says that love will never fail. When you show people that you love them, it will never fail. The love that you show them will draw them to GOD every time. You can show them Prophecies, tongues, or share your knowledge with them, but that may fail. But love will never fail. That is why GOD wants to give you total restoration in love. Because love never fails.

If you allow yourself to do it, GOD will give you total restoration in love. GOD will perfect HIS love in you and teach you how to love at all times, just the way HE does.

Then you will be able to bring other people to GOD, so that HE can give them total restoration in their lives the way HE wants to. That, my friend, is what total restoration is all about, and now is the time for us to allow GOD to give us total restoration in every area of our lives.

GOD loves you, and HE wants to change everything in you that would hinder your relationship with HIM, and with others.

GOD wants to give you a complete makeover in every area of your life. GOD wants to take away the bad, and restore it with good. And the first thing HE wants to start with is love. GOD wants to take everything in your life that will keep HIS love from being perfected in you, and GOD wants to give you total restoration in love.

GOD wants to give you total restoration in every area of your life, and HE wants to start in love. So, I say to you today, accept the love that GOD is offering you. Accept the Word of GOD in your life and start applying it to your life. Accept GOD'S total restoration in your life today.

Then you will be able to live that abundant, victorious life that Jesus wants you to live, and enjoy the Bible's full rewards.

That, my friend, is "Total Restoration."

Glory to God!

Chapter Three

Total Restoration in Joy

22.) But the fruit of the Spirit is love, joy, peace, longsuffering, gentleness, goodness, faith,

23.) Meekness, temperance: against such there is no law. GALATIANS 5:22-23

Praise GOD! My dear Christian friend, the second thing that GOD wants to give you total restoration in is your joy. GOD wants to give you total restoration in joy, and now is the time for you to allow GOD to do it.

GOD does not want you to walk around sad or unhappy all of the time. GOD wants you to have joy in your life. Joy is the second thing mentioned in the Fruit of the Spirit. So joy is the second thing that GOD wants to give you total restoration in.

If you have joy in your life, you can tell others of GOD'S goodness joyfully. And everybody wants to be happy and have joy in their lives. So when you share your joy with them and tell them that GOD is the reason you are so joyful, it will help you to win them over to GOD.

Jesus wants to fulfill HIS joy in us. HE wants our joy to be full and complete. Let's look at a verse to prove this.

And now come I to thee; and these things I speak in the world, that they might have my joy fulfilled in themselves.

JOHN 17:13

So you see, Jesus wants HIS joy to be fulfilled in us. That is good news my friend. GOD wants to give us total restoration in joy, and now is the time for us to allow HIM to do it.

GOD wants your joy to be full. So if your joy can be full, that means that you can have joy all of the time. Let's look at a verse to prove this.

Hitherto have ye asked nothing in my name: ask and ye shall receive, that your joy may be full.

JOHN 16:24

Praise GOD! My friend this is a powerful verse. Jesus said for us to ask for something in HIS name and we would get it, so that our joy would be full. GOD wants our joy to be full and complete. That is what total restoration in joy is all about, and now is the time for it.

GOD wants to restore joy to you. Satan will try to take your joy by getting you to sin. So if you are living for GOD and you have no joy, something may be wrong. Let's look at a verse to prove that GOD wants to restore your joy.

Restore unto me the joy of thy Salvation; and uphold me with thy free Spirit.

PSALMS 51:12

In this verse, King David had lost his joy because of sin. But he knew in his heart that GOD would restore his joy, so he asked GOD to restore it. GOD does want to give us total restoration in joy. GOD does not want us walking around sad all of the time. HE wants us to be happy. That is great news, to know that we do not have to be sad all of the time, and that GOD wants us to have joy instead of sadness.

GOD wants to give us joy for our mourning and sadness. HE wants to replace anything in our lives that keeps us down, with full, complete joy. Let's look at a verse to prove this.

To appoint unto them that mourn in Zion, to give unto them beauty for ashes, the oil of joy for mourning, the garment of Praise for the Spirit of heaviness; that they might be called trees of righteousness, the Planting of the Lord, that he might be glorified.

ISAIAH 61:3

This is a wonderful verse that proves that GOD wants to give us total restoration in every area of our lives. It shows that GOD wants to replace all the bad in our lives with good. It says that GOD wants to give us the oil of joy for our mourning and sadness. The oil of joy is the joy mentioned in the Fruit of the Spirit. GOD wants to take away everything in our lives that keeps us down, and replace it with all the good things that we need, to live an abundant, victorious life. GOD does want to give us total restoration in joy, and HE wants to do it now.

GOD does not want us sad all of the time. GOD wants to trade us joy for our tears. Let's look at a verse to prove this.

They that sow in tears shall reap in joy.

PSALMS 126:5

This verse shows us that GOD wants to give us joy for our tears. It is without a doubt GOD'S desire to give us total restoration in every area of our lives.

Satan will try his best to keep us down in every area of our lives, and GOD wants us to have an abundant, victorious life in every area of our lives. That is what total restoration is all about, and now is the time for it.

GOD wants to give us fullness of joy and pleasures in every area of our lives. Let's look at a verse to prove this.

Thou wilt shew me the path of life: in thy Presence is fulness of joy; at thy right hand there are Pleasures for evermore.

PSALMS 16:11

So you see, in GOD'S Presence, there is fullness of joy, and he wants to give us that fullness of joy. This verse also says that in GOD'S hands, there are pleasures for evermore. That is what total restoration is all about. Total restoration is about GOD taking away all of the bad in our lives, and replacing it with all the good and pleasure.

The Word of GOD says that we may weep at times, but GOD will restore our joy. So there may be times that we have to cry, but GOD will heal our heart's and restore our joy. Let's look at a verse to prove this.

For his anger endureth but for a moment; in his favour is life: Weeping may endure for a night, but joy cometh in the morning.
PSALMS 30:5

So, you see, the Word of GOD says that weeping may endure for a night, but joy will come in the morning. We may cry sometimes, but GOD will restore our joy as soon as it is over. This verse also shows us that GOD does not want us down and out all of the time, and it shows that GOD wants to restore to us joy for our weeping. Praise GOD! My friend, that is what total restoration is all about, and now is the time for us to allow GOD to give us total restoration in every area of our lives.

My dear Christian friend, you do not have to live a sad, defeated life anymore. The Word of GOD tells us that GOD has everything we need to live an abundant, victorious life in every area of our life.

Satan wants to keep us down in every area of our lives, and GOD wants to give us an abundant, victorious life in every area of our lives.

GOD wants to give us total restoration in every area of our lives. Right now, HE wants to give us total restoration in joy. So, I encourage everyone to accept what the Word of GOD says about it, and allow GOD to give us that total restoration in joy now.

Then you will be able to live that abundant, victorious life that Jesus wants you to live, and enjoy the Bible's full rewards.

That, my friend, is "Total Restoration."

Praise the Lord!

Chapter Four

Total Restoration in Peace

22.) But the fruit of The Spirit is love, joy, peace, longsuffering, gentleness, goodness, faith,

23.) Meekness, temperance: against such there is now law.

GALATIANS 5:22-23

My dear Christian friend, the next thing GOD wants to give you total restoration in is your peace.

Everybody wants peace in their lives. The world is crying out for peace, but true lasting peace can only come from GOD.

Jesus said that in HIM we should have peace, but in the world, we would have tribulation. Let's look at a verse to prove this.

Those things I have spoken unto you, that in me ye might have peace. In the world ye shall have tribulation: but be of good cheer; I have overcome the world.

JOHN 16:33

So, you see, if you are rooted and grounded in Jesus Christ, you will have true peace in your lives. It is when you step out of Christ and into the world that Satan and his unclean army will bombard you with tribulation, and try to steal the peace that GOD wishes for you to walk in. GOD wants to give you total restoration in peace, and the time for it is now.

Praise the LORD, my dear Christian friend, the Word of GOD says that we can also have peace with GOD. That means that you no longer have to worry about GOD waiting around the corner with a baseball bat to smack you every time you mess up, because we can have true peace with GOD. Let's look at a verse to prove this.

Therefore, being justified by faith, we have peace with God through our Lord Jesus Christ:

ROMANS 5:1

So, you see, there it is again, we have peace with GOD through our LORD Jesus Christ. That is right in line with the other verse that I gave you that said in Jesus Christ we will have peace. So, you see, according to this verse, in Christ we can have peace with Almighty GOD. Isn't that great my friend? You no longer have to live life worrying all the time or being uncertain about any and everything, because it is a promise right there in the Word of GOD, that we can have peace with GOD. GOD wants to give you total restoration in peace, and the time for it is now.

GOD also wants us to have peace in our homes. HE wants us to not only have peace in our homes, but prosperity as well. Let's look at a verse to prove this.

Peace be within thy walls, and Prosperity within thy Palaces.

PSALMS 122:7

So, you see, this verse says peace be within your walls. That means in your home, at your workplace, anywhere you may be, and in every area of your life. According to this verse, GOD wants us to have peace within our walls and prosperity within our Palaces. Glory to GOD! Take time today to just consider and thank GOD for your peace. GOD wants to give you total restoration in peace, and the time for it is now.

My dear Christian friend, not only does GOD want you to have peace, HE wants you to have perfect peace. The way to have that perfect peace is to keep your mind on GOD and trust in HIM. GOD wants to give you total restoration in peace, and HE wants to give you perfect peace. Let's look at a verse to prove this.

Thou wilt keep him in perfect peace, whose mind is stayed on thee: because he trusteth in thee.

ISAIAH 26:3

Glory to GOD! My dear Christian friend, GOD will give you perfect peace if you will keep your mind on HIM, and simply trust in HIM to do it. GOD wants to give you total restoration in peace, and the time for it is now.

So, my friend the next time that old toothless devil tries to steal your peace, you can just boldly proclaim that he is not taking your peace because you have perfect peace, and your mind is stayed on GOD and you trust in HIM.

Let me be the first to warn you that Satan and his unclean army is going to do everything in their power to steal your peace. That is all they are good for is to steal, kill, and destroy all peace for the Christian.

But the good news is, that you don't have to give in to them. You don't have to be troubled or afraid that the devil will steal your peace, because GOD gave it to you, and even told you not to be troubled or afraid, because you have it. Let's look at a verse to prove this.

Peace I leave with you, my peace I give unto you: not as the world giveth, give I unto you. Let not your heart be troubled, neither let it be afraid.

JOHN 14:27

So, you see, Jesus said that he gives us HIS peace. Not the kind of peace that the world has, but HIS perfect peace. The kind that GOD gives, and the devil can't take it from you. So don't let your heart be troubled, or be afraid of anybody taking it from you, because it is yours from GOD; bottom line, no one can take it from you. Glory to GOD!

GOD wants to give you total restoration in peace that no one can take from you, and the time for it is now.

My dear Christian friend, did you know that Jesus Christ our LORD and Savior, and our Mighty King of kings is even referred to as the Prince of Peace? HE is our Prince that imparts HIS glorious peace into our lives. Let's look at a verse to prove this.

For unto us a child is born, unto us a Son is given: and the government shall be upon his shoulder: and his name shall be called Wonderful, Counsellor, The Mighty God, The Everlasting Father, The Prince of Peace.

ISAIAH 9:6

So, you see, even one of HIS Names is called The Prince of Peace, my dear Christian friend, Jesus Christ is our Prince of Peace, and HE wants to give us HIS peace in every area of our lives, and it is a perfect peace that no one, not even that old toothless devil, can take it from us. Praise the LORD! GOD wants to give us total restoration in peace, and the time for it is now. So just humble yourself and submit to GOD; let HIM, the one and only Jesus Christ, The King of kings and LORD of lords, the Mighty Prince of Peace, bless you with HIS perfect peace in every area of your life. Let HIM give you peace in your homes, let HIM give you peace in your finances, let HIM give you peace in your relationships and friendships, let HIM give you peace in your everyday life, let HIM give you peace when you are asleep, and peace when you are awake. Praise GOD, just let HIM bestow HIS abundant peace on you in every area of your life. GOD wants to give you total restoration in peace, and the time for it is now.

My dear Christian friend, if you will just make up your mind to allow GOD to give you total restoration in peace, HE will impart HIS peace within you and that is a perfect peace which passes all understanding. You will have such powerful peace, you won't even be able to understand it, nor will the people you come in contact with. Let's look at a verse to prove this.

And the Peace of God, which passeth all understanding, shall keep your hearts and minds through Christ Jesus.

PHILIPPIANS 4:7

So, you see, GOD wants to give you a peace that passes all understanding, and it will be a perfect peace that will keep your hearts and your minds through Christ Jesus. Praise GOD, that is good news. GOD wants to give you total restoration in peace, and the time for it is now.

So, I say to you my friend, allow GOD to give you total restoration in peace here and now. It is here and it is yours, it is available for you right this very minute.

Allow GOD to give you total restoration in peace now.

Then you will be able to live that abundant, victorious life that Jesus wants you to live, and enjoy the Bible's full rewards.

That, my friend, is "Total Restoration."

Thank you, Jesus!

Chapter Five

Total Restoration in Long-Suffering

22.) But the fruit of the Spirit is love, joy, peace, longsuffering, gentleness, goodness, faith,

23.) Meekness, temperance: against such there is no law.

GALATIANS 5:22-23

My dear Christian friend, the next thing GOD wants to give you total restoration in is longsuffering. The very best word to describe longsuffering is simply Patience.

My friend, the world is in dire need of Patience. It sometimes seems that no one wants to even drive someplace, because they don't have the patience to drive on the street with other drivers, or even wait for a caution or red light to change.

People today may not have the patience to stand in a store line, or wait for even gas for their car. The world is in dire need for patience.

But let me give you some good news, GOD wants to give you total restoration in patience, and HE wants to do it now.

Did you know that the Word of GOD tells us to be followers of those who through faith and patience, inherit the promises? So according to the Word of GOD, it takes faith and patience to inherit GOD'S Promises. Let's look at a verse to prove this.

That ye be not slothful, but followers of them who through faith and patience inherit the promises.

HEBREWS 6:12

So, you see, there it is from the Word of GOD, that we inherit the promises through faith and patience.

My dear Christian friend, GOD'S Word is full of promises for each and every one of us.

You see, Satan and his unclean army will try to steal your patience to keep you from inheriting the promises of GOD. He will do everything in his power to keep you from getting GOD'S Promises in your life.

But the good news for you today is that GOD wants to give you total restoration in patience, and the time for it is now.

My dear Christian friend, the Word of GOD is clear about you and I having patience. It even tells us to follow after patience. Let's look at a verse to prove this.

But thou, O man of God, flee these things; and follow after righteousness, godliness, faith, love, patience, and meekness.

1st TIMOTHY 6:11

So, you see, there it is again in the Word of GOD, telling us to flee other things of the world, and follow after patience. This is showing us clearly that GOD wants us to have total restoration in patience, and the time for it is now.

I can tell you how patience comes. It comes when your faith is tried. Let's look at a verse to prove this.

Knowing this, that the trying of your faith worketh patience.

JAMES 1:3

So, you see, when old Satan tries your faith, and you just keep patiently waiting for the promises of GOD to be manifested in your life, you will without a doubt eventually inherit the Promises of GOD. GOD'S Word says it, and that settles it, you will have the Promises of GOD, if you'll just be patient.

Glory to GOD! That is good news my dear Christian friend. It is a fact that GOD wants to give you total restoration in patience, and the time for it is now.

Let me tell you dear Christian, if you will allow GOD to impart HIS patience in you, and you inherit the Promises of GOD, you will want for nothing.

Let's look at a verse to prove this.

But let patience have her perfect work, that ye may be perfect and entire, wanting nothing.

JAMES 1:4

Glory to GOD, Praise the LORD! According to this verse, if we will just let patience have her perfect work in us, we will want for nothing. That is because when we let patience have her perfect work, we will inherit the Promises of GOD, and we will want for nothing. That is good news my dear Christian friend. GOD wants to give you total restoration in Patience, and the time for it is now.

My dear Christian friend, the Word of GOD tells us to be patient, for the coming of the LORD is drawing near.

Let's look at a verse to prove this.

Be ye also Patient; establish your hearts: for the coming of the Lord draweth nigh.

JAMES 5:8

I know you have heard many, many times that Jesus is coming soon. Let me tell you if you will just be patient, that is another mighty promise from the Word of GOD that you will inherit, because it is a promise that Jesus Christ is coming again, and oh what a glorious day that will be. I don't know about you, but I want the patience to wait and inherit that mighty promise, and I know you do to.

My dear Christian friend, it is a fact that GOD wants to give you total restoration in patience, and I say to you, the time for it is now.

You see my friend; the Word of GOD is full of promises for you. And I can tell you that you will need patience to wait to inherit those promises.

Satan and his unclean army will try to steal your patience to keep you from inheriting the Promises of GOD.

But if you will just have hope. Find out what the Word of GOD says concerning anything you need in life and just hope for it, and wait in patience for it, you will want for nothing.

Let's look at a verse to prove this.

But if we hope for that we see not, then do we with Patience wait for it.

ROMANS 8:25

So, you see, if you will just allow GOD to impart HIS patience in you, then you will be able to wait for HIS promises to come to you. HE will bless you with all of HIS promises and you will want for nothing. Praise the LORD! GOD wants to give you total restoration in patience, and the time for it is now.

My dear Christian friend, you may be trying to witness to someone, maybe it is someone you love, and you really want to see them saved. Don't give up on them whatever you do, because the Word of GOD says that we bring forth fruit with patience.

Just think, if GOD had given up on us, we would be in big trouble. But GOD brought us forth with patience. And that is how we Christians bear fruit, we do it with patience, until the person we are witnessing to finally accepts what we are saying.

Let's look at a verse to prove this.

But that on the good ground are they, which in an honest and good heart, having heard the word, keep it, and bring forth fruit with Patience.

LUKE 8:15

So, you see, the way we bring forth fruit is with patience. When you want to witness to someone, just speak to them in love, and do it with patience, and you will win them over to Christ every time. Glory to GOD! My friend, GOD wants to give you total restoration in patience so you can witness and bring people to know Jesus Christ. You will bear fruit with patience.

My dear Christian friend, GOD wants to give you total restoration in patience, and the time for it is now.

So, I say to you, humble yourself today and allow GOD to impart HIS patience in you, and you will without a doubt begin to inherit the Promises of GOD in your life. And before you know it, you will want for nothing. Praise the LORD!

Allow GOD to give you total restoration in patience now.

Then you will be able to live that abundant, victorious life that Jesus wants you to live, and enjoy the Bible's full rewards.

That, my friend, is "Total Restoration."

Hallelujah!

Chapter Six

Total Restoration in Gentleness

22.) But the fruit of the Spirit is love, joy, peace, longsuffering, gentleness, goodness, faith,

23.) Meekness, temperance, against such there is no law.

GALATIANS 5:22-23

My dear Christian friend, the next thing GOD wants to give you total restoration in is gentleness.

We all need gentleness in our lives. Especially since we are still on Earth, and we have to deal with people in our everyday lives.

My dear Christian friend, GOD is a very gentle loving GOD, HE abounds with gentleness, and HE wants to impart HIS gentleness in us. HIS gentleness will without a doubt make us great, if it abounds in our lives.

Let's look at a verse to prove this.

Thou hast also given me the shield of thy Salvation: and thy gentleness hath made me great.

2nd SAMUEL 22:36

Praise the LORD! My dear Christian friend, according to that verse, GOD'S gentleness will make us great. That is because if it abounds in our lives, it will bring glory to GOD, and we will become great in the Kingdom of GOD, which will in turn bring us greatness and favor in the world as well. Praise the LORD! GOD wants to give us total restoration in gentleness, and the time for it is now.

You see, when we allow GOD to impart HIS gentleness in our lives, it will help us to become humble and kind in every area of our lives. You may need gentleness when you're standing in a store line and the person behind you is making every effort to say something negative concerning the store clerk being slow or something to that nature. That is when you allow your gentleness to kick in, and you could even go as far as to tell the store clerk that they are doing a great job, and to keep the change for a tip. That would shame the old toothless devil, and make you great in the Kingdom of GOD. Praise the LORD! My dear Christian friend, GOD wants to give us total restoration in gentleness, and the time for us to allow HIM to do it is now.

Have you ever wondered how you can become great in the Kingdom of GOD? It is simple, just allow GOD to impart HIS gentleness in your life, and let it abound in everything you do. Let your gentleness abound in your home, with your family, with your friends, in your workplace, when you're out shopping or just picking up a little milk from the store, let your gentleness abound in your Church, let is abound in your everyday life, in everything you do. Glory to GOD! My dear friend, GOD wants to give you total restoration in a humble gentleness that will make you great, and the time for us to allow HIM to do it is now.

The very same verse that I gave you earlier showing that GOD'S gentleness would make you great, is used again in the Book of PSALMS, and it says that GOD'S gentleness will make us great. That is why GOD wants to restore gentleness in our lives. Let's look at the same verse, but in another book of the Bible to prove this.

Thou hast also given me the shield of thy Salvation: and thy right hand hath holden me up, and thy gentleness hath made me great.

PSALMS 18:35

So, you see, there it is again, right from the Word of GOD, showing us clearly that GOD'S gentleness will make us great. Glory to GOD! GOD wants to give us total restoration in gentleness, and the time for it is now.

My dear Christian friend, Jesus Christ allowed gentleness to abound in HIS life when HE was here on Earth. Just read the Gospels, and you will see how gentleness did abound in the life of our Mighty Great King of kings and Lord of lords, Jesus Christ. There is no doubt that we can still abound in the gentleness of Jesus Christ here and now, even though HE is sitting at the right hand of GOD.

That is good news my dear friend. It is a fact that GOD wants to give us total restoration in gentleness, and the time for us to allow HIM to do it is now. Let's look at a verse to prove that we can abound in the gentleness of Jesus Christ.

Now I Paul myself beseech you by the meekness and gentleness of Christ, who in Presence am base among you, but being absent am bold toward you:

2nd CORINTHIANS 10:1

In this verse, Paul, the man of GOD, who wrote most of our New Testament Scriptures, spoke to us in the meekness and gentleness of Christ. Glory to GOD! The Word of GOD speaks to us in gentleness to impart GOD'S gentleness in us, and it is a gentleness that will make us great in the Kingdom of GOD, and bring glory to HIS name. Praise the LORD! GOD wants to give us total restoration in gentleness, and the time for us to allow HIM to do it is now.

The Apostle Paul learned to allow gentleness to abound in his life. That is how GOD used him to write most of our New Testament, because Paul saw that GOD wanted to impart total restoration in his life. So, he allowed GOD to impart gentleness in his life, and he allowed it to abound in his life. So, GOD used him in a mighty way. Let's look at a verse to show that Paul allowed gentleness to abound in his life.

But we were gentle among you, even as a nurse Cherisheth her children:

1st THESSALONIANS 2:7

In this verse, Paul said that he allowed gentleness to abound in his life so much that he even compared his gentleness to that of the way a nurse cherishes children.

Paul allowed gentleness to abound in his life, and it made him great. Glory to GOD! Paul became great and wrote most of our New Testament, simply because he allowed GOD to impart gentleness in his life, and he allowed it to abound in everything he did. Praise the LORD! GOD wants to give us total restoration in gentleness, and the time for it is now.

My dear Christian friend, the Word of GOD is clear to us, that we as Servants of The LORD are to be gentle, and allow gentleness to abound in our lives to other people we come in contact with.

Let's look at a verse to prove this.

And the Servant of the Lord must not strive; but be gentle unto all men, apt to teach, Patient,

2nd TIMOTHY 2:24

So, you see, according to this verse, we are told to be gentle to all men. We are to allow gentleness to abound in our lives, and when we do, it will without a doubt make us great in the Kingdom of GOD. Praise the LORD! GOD wants to give us total restoration in gentleness, and the time for us to allow HIM to do it is now.

Let me be the first to tell you that Satan and his unclean army will do everything they can to keep you from being gentle, that is because he knows if you allow gentleness to abound in your life, it will make you great in the Kingdom of GOD. Satan may bring a hateful, mean person across your path, but no matter how hateful or mean that person may be, you can still be gentle to them. When you are gentle to other people, it will humble them.

If you are witnessing to someone, do it in gentleness, and you will win them over to GOD every time.

Praise the LORD! My dear Christian friend, GOD wants to give you total restoration in a gentleness that will make you great in the Kingdom of GOD, and help you win souls over to Christ, and the time for us to allow HIM to do it is now.

So, I say to you, humble yourself and allow GOD to give you total restoration in gentleness today. Then you will be able to live that abundant, victorious life that Jesus wants you to live, and enjoy the Bible's full rewards.

That, my friend, is "Total Restoration."

Glory to GOD!

Chapter Seven

Total Restoration in Goodness

22.) But the fruit of the Spirit is love, joy, peace, longsuffering, gentleness, goodness, faith,

23.) Meekness, temperance: against such there is no law.

GALATIANS 5:22-23

Praise the LORD! My dear Christian friend, the next thing GOD wants to give you total restoration in is goodness.

My dear Christian friend, GOD is a good GOD, and HE wants to impart HIS goodness into you. GOD wants to give us total restoration in goodness and the time for it is now.

My friend, in the Word of GOD, Moses asked GOD to show him HIS glory. But GOD is so great, that Moses could not look fully at GOD'S face, so GOD just allowed Moses to see HIS goodness.

Let's look at a verse to prove this.

And he said, I will make all my goodness pass before thee, and I will proclaim the name of the Lord before thee; and I will be gracious to whom I will be gracious, and will shew mercy on whom I will shew mercy.

EXODUS 33:19

Moses was a great Man of GOD, and GOD allowed Moses to see all of HIS goodness. What a great blessing that must have been for Moses. The same can apply to you and me today my friend, we can see all of the goodness of GOD here and now. GOD wants to impart HIS goodness in us here and now. Praise the LORD! GOD wants to give us total restoration in goodness, and the time for it is now.

My dear friend, when the LORD actually passed by Moses to show him HIS goodness, GOD, Himself proclaimed that HE was abundant in goodness.

Let's look at a verse to prove this.

And the Lord passed by before him, and proclaimed, The Lord, The Lord God, merciful and gracious, longsuffering, and abundant in goodness and truth. EXODUS 34:6

So, you see, GOD is abundant in goodness, and HE wants to impart HIS goodness in us here and now. Praise the LORD! GOD wants to give us total restoration in abundant goodness, just as HE is, and the time for it is now.

As I said, GOD is a good GOD, and we are to rejoice in HIS goodness. Let's look at a verse to prove this.

Now therefore arise, O Lord God, into thy resting place, thou, and the ark of thy strength: let thy Priests, O Lord God, be clothed with Salvation, and let thy Saints rejoice in goodness.

2nd CHRONICLES 6:41

So, you see, according to this verse, we are to allow GOD to impart HIS goodness in us, and Praise GOD, we are to rejoice in that goodness. GOD is a good GOD, and HE wants to give us total restoration in goodness, and the time for it is now.

My dear Christian friend, if you are hungry for it, GOD will fill you with goodness. It is a fact that GOD wants to give you total restoration in goodness, and the time for it is now.

Let's look at a verse to prove that if you are hungry for goodness, GOD desires to fill you with it.

For he satisfieth the longing soul, and filleth the hungry soul with goodness.

PSALMS 107:9

My dear Christian friend, I don't know about you, but I'm hungry and I want GOD to fill me with HIS goodness. GOD desires to fill us with HIS goodness to the point that it will abound in our lives in everything we do.

According to this verse, if you are longing for it, GOD will satisfy you with it, and if you are hungry for it, GOD will fill you with it. Praise the LORD! GOD wants to fill us and give us total restoration in goodness, and the time for it is now.

Mt dear Christian friend, the Word of GOD says that we should Praise the LORD for HIS goodness.

Let's look at a verse to prove this.

Oh, that men would Praise the Lord for His goodness, and for His wonderful works to the Children of men!

PSALMS 107:15

So, you see, we are to Praise the LORD for HIS goodness. The more we Praise HIM for goodness, the more HE will impart it unto us, and fill us with HIS very own goodness. Praise the LORD! GOD wants to give us total restoration in goodness, and the time for it is now.

My dear Christian friend, I exhort you to allow GOD to impart HIS goodness in you, and continue in it. The Word of GOD actually says that if you do not continue in the goodness of GOD, you may be cut off.

Let's look at a verse to prove this.

Behold therefore the goodness and severity of God: on them which fell, severity; but toward thee, goodness, if thou continue in his goodness: otherwise, thou also shalt be cut off.

ROMANS 11:22

My dear Christian friend, according to this verse, if you do not continue in HIS goodness, you could be cut off. So, you see, this verse is one of the main reasons GOD wants to impart HIS goodness in us, it is so we won't be cut off. I don't know about you, but I don't think I want to be cut off, so I think I had just rather continue in goodness. It is a fact that GOD wants to give us total restoration in goodness, and the time for it is now.

My dear Christian friend, Jesus Himself referred to Himself as the Good Shepherd, and GOD wants to impart HIS goodness in us.

Let's look at a verse to prove this.

I am the good Shepherd: the good Shepherd giveth his life for the sheep.

JOHN 10:11

My dear Christian friend, it was a good thing that Jesus gave HIS life for us. If HE had not have done that good deed, we would all be lost without hope. But Praise the LORD, since Jesus is the Good Shepherd, and HE gave HIS life for us, now HE wants us to follow HIS example and be good. GOD wants to give us total restoration in goodness, and the time for it is now.

My dear Christian friend, if you will allow GOD to impart HIS goodness in you, then you can actually be a good Minister of the LORD Jesus Christ.

Let's look at a verse to prove this.

If thou put the brethren in remembrance of these things, thou shalt be a good minister of Jesus Christ, nourished up in the words of faith and of good doctrine, whereunto thou hast attained.

1st TIMOTHY 4:6

Praise the LORD! My dear Christian friend, if you will allow GOD to impart HIS goodness in you, and allow it to abound in your life, you can actually become a good Minister of Jesus Christ. Praise the LORD! GOD wants to give you total restoration in a goodness that will without a doubt make you a good Minister of Jesus Christ, and the time for us to allow HIM to do it is now.

My dear Christian friend, it is my whole heart's desire that you will allow GOD to impart HIS good in you, so that one day you will hear the LORD say well done good and faithful Servant, enter into the joy of the LORD. That is why GOD wants to impart HIS goodness in us, so that one day HE will be able to say to us "well done good and faithful Servant, enter into the joy of the LORD."

Let's look at a verse to prove this.

His lord said unto him, well done, thou good and faithful Servant: thou hast been faithful over a few things, I will make thee ruler over many things: enter thou into the joy of thy lord.

MATTHEW 25:21

Praise the LORD! My dear Christian friend, GOD wants to give us total restoration in goodness, so that one day HE can say to us "well done good and faithful Servant, enter into the joy of thy LORD."

GOD wants to give us total restoration in goodness, and the time for it is now.

I exhort you today to allow GOD to give you total restoration in goodness.

Then you will be able to live that abundant, victorious life that Jesus wants you to live, and enjoy The Bible's full rewards.

That, my friend, is "Total Restoration!"

Praise the LORD!

Chapter Eight

Total Restoration in Faith

22.) But the fruit of the Spirit is love, joy, peace, longsuffering, gentleness, goodness, faith,

23.) Meekness, temperance: against such there is no law.

GALATIANS 5:22-23

My dear Christian friend, the next thing GOD wants to give you total restoration in is faith.

You will need faith in your relationship with GOD to please HIM. GOD wants to take away your doubt, and unbelief and fears that GOD will not or is not able to give you an abundant, victorious life, or anything else and replace that with a good strong, solid faith in HIM. GOD wants to give you total restoration in faith, and the time for you to allow HIM to do it is now.

We know that GOD wants us to have faith, because the Word of GOD says that it is impossible to please GOD without faith.

Let's look at a verse to prove this.

But without faith it is impossible to please him: for he that cometh to God must believe that he is, and that he is a rewarder of them that diligently seek him.

HEBREWS 11:6

So, you see, this proves that GOD wants us to have faith, because GOD always wants us to please HIM. We all need faith to please GOD. It also says that those who come to GOD must believe that HE is, and that means that we must believe that HE is everything we need in life, that HE is a good GOD, that HE is a faithful GOD, that HE is well able to give us an abundant, victorious life in every area of our lives, and that HE is able to give us total restoration in faith right now.

The Word of GOD also says that we walk by faith, that means that we live it. We walk it, we talk it, we do not doubt it, we proclaim it, everything we do, we do by our faith.

Let's look at a verse to prove this.

For we walk by faith, not by sight:

2nd CORINTHIANS 5:7

So, you see, according to this verse, we walk by faith, not by sight. That means that we live faith, that we talk faith, that we practice it in our lives to live that abundant, victorious life that GOD wants us to live. My dear friend, GOD wants to give you total restoration in faith, and the time for all of us to allow HIM to do it is now.

Let me tell you something, Satan will try every trick in the book to get you to doubt GOD. Satan wants us to be weak in faith, because he knows that if we are weak in faith, we cannot please GOD. But Glory to GOD, faith is a shield for us that will stop old Satan in his tracks.

Let's look at a verse to prove this.

Above all taking the shield of faith, wherewith ye shall be able to quench all the fiery darts of the wicked.

EPHESIANS 6:16

This verse plainly says that faith is a shield, and not only that, but it is a shield that will quench "all" the fiery darts of the wicked. Satan will come at you with everything he can to steal your faith. But it is your faith that will shield off anything he brings at you. You can use the very faith that Satan is trying to take from you, and use it to defeat that old toothless devil. Praise the LORD! GOD wants to give you total restoration in faith, and the time for it is now.

My dear Christian friend, GOD wants all of HIS People to be strong in faith. The Bible says that Abraham was strong in faith, and in that he was giving glory to GOD.

Let's look at a verse to prove this.

He staggered not at the Promise of God through unbelief; but was strong in faith giving glory to God;

ROMANS 4:20

This verse shows us a good example of how GOD wants all of us to be strong in faith. It shows here that Abraham did not doubt the Promise of GOD, or have unbelief; and the very reason he didn't, is because he was strong in faith, and GOD wants all of us to be strong in faith, just like Abraham. My dear friend, GOD wants to give us total restoration in faith, and HE wants us to be strong in it, and the time for us to allow HIM to do it is now.

Let me tell you how faith comes, according to the Word of GOD, faith comes by hearing, and the hearing mentioned here is the Word of GOD itself. The more you hear the Word of GOD, the stronger you will be in faith.

Let's look at a verse to prove this.

So, then faith cometh by hearing, and hearing by the word of God.

ROMANS 10:17

So, you see, it says faith comes by hearing, and hearing by the Word of GOD. So, the more you hear the Word of GOD, the stronger you will be in faith. The Word of GOD will bring you total restoration in faith if you will read it, study it, live it, and apply it to every area of your life. My dear friend, GOD wants to give you total restoration in faith, and now is the time for it.

My dear Christian friend, all of the things GOD wants to give us total restoration in, work together in our lives to make us better Christians. The very word Christian means to be Christ-like, and the very reason GOD wants to give us total restoration in every area of our lives, is to make us more Christ-like. But everything I have mentioned thus far concerning the things GOD wants to totally restore us in, works together in our lives to make us more Christ-like. Like faith works by love. We need the love to have faith, and the faith to have love, and the love to have joy and so forth. Let's look at a verse to prove that faith works by love.

For in Jesus Christ neither circumcision availeth anything, nor un-circumcision, but faith which worketh by love.

GALATIANS 5:6

So, you see, according to the last part of this verse, faith works by love. So, we need love to have strong faith, we need faith to have strong love, we need both of them to have joy. We need a balance of all of these things mentioned in this book. So we can live that abundant, victorious life that GOD wants us to live, and so we will be more Christ-like.

My dear friend, GOD wants to give us total restoration in faith, and the time to allow HIM to do it is now.

My dear Christian friend, we need faith to overcome the devil and the world and everything in the world that would hinder us from becoming more Christ-like.

Let's look at a verse to prove this.

For whatsoever is born of God overcometh the world: and this is the victory that overcometh the world, even our faith.

1st JOHN 5:4

So, you see, it is our faith that overcomes the world and helps us to live that abundant, victorious life that GOD wants us to live. So, we need faith to be overcomers and live that abundant, victorious life that GOD wants us to live, we need faith to please GOD, we need faith to quench all the fiery darts of the devil. My dear friend it is a fact we need faith, and GOD wants us to have it. GOD wants to give us total restoration in faith, and the time for it is now.

My dear Christian friend, Jesus is the Author and Finisher of faith. HE wants to give us total restoration in faith, and HE wants to complete it.

Let's look at a verse to prove this.

Looking unto Jesus the author and finisher of our faith; who for the joy that was set before him endured the Cross, despising the shame, and is set down at the right hand of the throne of God.

Hebrews 12:2

Praise the LORD! The first part of this verse says that Jesus is the author and finisher of our faith. Jesus wants to give us total restoration in faith, and the time for us to allow HIM to do it is now.

So, I encourage you today to allow Jesus to give you total restoration in faith, so you can live that life of victory, and be an overcomer.

Then you will be able to live that abundant, victorious life that Jesus wants you to live, and enjoy the Bible's full rewards.

That, my friend, is "Total Restoration."

Glory to GOD!

Chapter Nine

Total Restoration in Meekness

22.) But the fruit of the Spirit is love, joy, peace, longsuffering, gentleness, goodness, faith,

23.) Meekness, temperance: against such there is no law.
GALATIANS 5:22-23

My dear Christian friend, the very next thing GOD wants to give us total restoration in is meekness.

To be meek means to be gentle and kind.

If you will read the Gospels, you will see clearly that Jesus is meek in everything HE does. So, the next thing GOD wants to give us total restoration in is meekness, and the time for us to allow HIM to do it is now.

My dear friend, the Word of GOD tells us to seek meekness, so that we may be hidden in the day of the LORD'S anger.

Let's look at a verse to prove this.

Seek ye the Lord, all ye meek of the earth, which have wrought his judgment; seek righteousness, seek meekness: it may be ye shall be hid in the day of the Lord's anger.
ZEPHANIAH 2:3

So, you see, we are to seek meekness. There may be times when Satan and his unclean army try to come against you, to keep you from being meek.

The devil may work through someone to make you angry. But the best thing to do is remain meek. A soft answer will turn anger away. So, to overcome the devil, we must remain meek.

Let me tell you dear friend, GOD will use you to witness for HIM if you are meek, and HE will use you in mighty ways.

Moses was very meek, and look how greatly the LORD used him.

Let's look at a verse to prove that Moses was very meek.

Now the man Moses was very meek, above all the men which were upon the face of the earth.

NUMBERS 12:3

According to this verse, Moses was meeker than all the men in the earth at that time. The LORD used Moses in mighty ways because Moses was so meek, and the LORD will use you in mighty ways if you will remain meek at all times.

My dear Christian friend, the Word of GOD says the meek shall eat and be satisfied, and Praise the LORD. That is because GOD can speak to you and get through to you if you will remain meek.

Let's look at a verse to prove that the meek shall eat and be satisfied.

The meek shall eat and be satisfied: they shall Praise the Lord that seek him: your heart shall live forever.

PSALMS 22:26

Praise GOD! Dear Christian friend, according to this verse, the meek shall eat and be satisfied.

That is because if you remain meek at all times, GOD will be the one who satisfies you.

My dear Christian friend, GOD wants to give us total restoration in meekness, and the time for us to allow HIM to do it is now.

You see, if you will remain meek, GOD will be able to guide you and teach you HIS ways. That is why GOD wants us to remain meek at all times.

Let's look at a verse to prove this.

The meek will he guide in judgment: and the meek will he teach his way.

PSALMS 25:9

So, you see, the Word of GOD says right there, that if you are meek, GOD will teach you HIS way and guide you.

You see, Satan and his unclean army does not want you to allow GOD to guide you, or for you to learn GOD'S way. The devil wants you to live his way, the evil way. But GOD wants you to live HIS way, but in order for GOD to teach you HIS way, you must remain meek. When you remain meek, GOD will bless you in every area of your life, and that old devil will just have to hang his head and leave you alone.

My dear Christian friend, the Word of GOD says the meek shall inherit the earth, and delight themselves in the abundance of peace. Glory to GOD! Don't that sound great my dear Christian friend?

Let's look at a verse to prove this.

But the meek shall inherit the earth; and shall delight themselves in the abundance of peace.

PSALMS 37:11

My dear Christian friend, if you want to inherit the earth and delight yourself in the abundance of peace, just remain meek. Remain meek with GOD, remain meek at your workplace, remain meek with your friends and loved ones, remain meek with your enemies; my dear Christian friend remain meek at all times, and you will be blessed abundantly.

My dear Christian friend, Jesus Himself said you are blessed if you are meek.

Let's look at a verse to prove this.

Blessed are the meek: for they shall inherit the earth.

MATTHEW 5:5

So, you see right there Jesus said, blessed are the meek. My dear Christian friend, GOD wants to give you total restoration in meekness, and the time for it is now.

My dear friend, the LORD will lift you up if you will remain meek. But as for the wicked, HE will cast them to the ground.

Let's look at a verse to prove this.

The Lord lifteth up the meek: he casteth the wicked down to the ground.

PSALMS 147:6

So, you see, according to this verse, The LORD will lift you up if you are meek. If you remain meek, the LORD will lift you up in your Ministry, the LORD will lift you up at your workplace, the LORD will lift you up with your family and friends, the LORD will lift you up in every area of your life, if you will remain meek and allow HIM to. Glory to GOD! GOD wants to give you total restoration in meekness so HE can lift you up, and the time for it is now.

Praise GOD! Dear people, the Word of GOD says GOD will beautify the meek with Salvation. That is because, if you are meek, you can hear the LORD when HE calls your name.

Let's look at a verse to prove this.

For the Lord taketh pleasure in his people: he will beautify the meek with Salvation.

PSALMS 149:4

My dear Christian friend, to be beautified with Salvation covers a lot. That is because Salvation means to be happy, have prosperity, to be delivered, it means to be sound and rescued, and just an altogether well-being. Praise the LORD! GOD wants to beautify you with Salvation and give you total restoration in meekness, and the time for us to allow HIM to do it is now.

My dear Christian friend, if you will remain meek, you will increase your joy in the LORD.

Let's look at a verse to prove this.

The meek also shall increase their joy in the Lord, and the poor among men shall rejoice in the Holy One of Israel.

ISAIAH 29:19

Praise GOD friend, if you will remain meek, GOD will increase your joy in the LORD, HE will beautify you with Salvation, and you will be blessed.

So, I say to you today, right now GOD wants to give us total restoration in meekness, so let's allow HIM to do it.

Humble yourself today, and allow GOD to give you total restoration in meekness, and you will be blessed.

Then you will be able to live that abundant, victorious life that Jesus wants you to live, and enjoy the Bible's full rewards.

That, my friend, is "Total Restoration!"

Praise the LORD!

Chapter Ten

Total Restoration in Temperance

22.) But the fruit of the Spirit is love, joy, peace, longsuffering, gentleness, goodness, faith,

23.) Meekness, temperance: against such there is no law.
GALATIANS 5:22-23

My dear Christian friend, the very next thing GOD wants to give you total restoration in is temperance.

Please allow me to define temperance for you. Temperance simply means self-control.

Let me assure you that you will need temperance in this life, in every area of your life.

Let me warn you that it is very easy to allow yourself to get out of control. See, Satan knows all of your weak points, and believe me, he will tempt you in every one of them to draw you away from GOD, and stop you from doing what GOD wants you to do.

Satan and his unclean army will tempt you in the things of the world. Things like drugs, sex, money, anything he can use to draw you away from GOD. But GOD wants to give you total restoration in temperance, so you can overcome all of those temptations Satan will bring your way.

Praise the LORD! GOD wants to give you total restoration in temperance, and the time for you to allow HIM to do it is now.

My dear Christian friend, you will need temperance to keep yourself from becoming complacent in the things you have adapted to in your lifetime. You may have become complacent in hating people, or being prejudice, or taking drugs, or doing things your way all the time. But GOD wants to impart temperance in you to replace that hate with love, HE wants to replace that prejudice with a sincere deep concern and love for everybody, HE wants to replace those drugs with healthy things, and HE wants to help you stop doing things your way, so you can learn to live HIS way.

Let me tell you, your flesh will not want you to have temperance, because that will mean you have to make some changes in your life.

In the Bible, Paul preached to a man named Felix about being in Christ, and temperance, and the man actually trembled concerning it. That is because he had become complacent in his own ways.

Let's look at a verse to prove this.

And as he reasoned of righteousness, temperance, and judgment to come, Felix trembled, and answered, Go thy way for this time; when I have a convenient season, I will call for thee.

ACTS 24:25

See Felix reasoned concerning temperance, in other words, he thought about it, and trembled. His answer shows that he had become complacent. He said, Go thy way for this time; and when I have a convenient season, I will call for thee.

Actually, what Felix was saying was, not right now, I am complacent in my ways, but when the time is right for me, when it is convenient, I will call for you, so I can make the changes I need concerning temperance. My dear Christian friend, you will need temperance to overcome all of the ungodly things in your life that you have adapted to, and to change your ways to GOD'S ways.

Praise the LORD! GOD wants to give you total restoration in temperance, and the time for you to allow HIM to do it is now.

You see, when you have no temperance, you may fall weak to any and every thing.

Let's look at a verse to prove this.

He that hath no rule over his own Spirit is like a city that is broken down, and without walls.

PROVERBS 25:28

What this verse is actually saying is, he who has no self-control, temperance, is weak and has no defense against Satan and his unclean armies, temptations, or the things of the world. If you don't have temperance, you will be weak, like a broken-down city, and without walls.

But, Praise the LORD, GOD wants to give you total restoration in temperance so you will be strong in every area of your life, and the time for you to allow HIM to do it is now.

You see, when you have temperance, GOD considers you better than mighty. You will actually become strong in GOD'S ways when you have temperance.

Let's look at a verse to prove this.

He that is slow to anger is better than the mighty; and he that ruleth his Spirit than he that taketh a city.

PROVERBS 16:32

My friend, according to this verse, if you are slow to anger, if you have temperance concerning your temper, GOD considers you to be better than the mighty. It also says that if you rule your Spirit yourself, you are better than one who takes a city.

In other words, if you will allow GOD to impart HIS temperance in you, and you have self-control, you will be mighty in all you do. If you have temperance, you will be mighty, but if you don't, you will be weak.

My dear Christian friend, Jesus is our best example of how to exercise temperance in our lives.

In MATTHEW Chapter 4, verses 1-10, Jesus had fasted for forty days and forty nights, and then the devil came to tempt HIM. The devil tempted Jesus in the areas that he thought Jesus was weak in. But Jesus exercised temperance every time the devil tempted HIM, and responded with the Word of GOD.

Let's look at these verses to prove this.

1.) Then was Jesus led up of the Spirit unto the wilderness to be tempted of the devil.

2.) And when he had fasted forty days and forty nights, he was afterward an hungered.

3.) And when the tempter came to him, he said, If thou be the Son of God, Command that these stones be made bread.

4.) But he answered and said, It is written, Man shall not live by bread alone, but by every word that Proceedeth out of the mouth of God.

5.) Then the devil taketh him up into the holy city, and setteth him on a Pinnacle of the temple,

6.) And saith unto him, if thou be the Son of God, cast thyself down: for it is written. He shall give his angels charge concerning thee: and in their hands they shall bear thee up, lest at any time thou dash thy foot against a stone.

7.) Jesus said unto him, It is written again, Thou shalt not tempt the Lord thy God.

8.) Again, the devil taketh him up into an exceeding high mountain, and sheweth him all the Kingdoms of the world, and the glory of them;

9.) And saith unto him, All these things will I give thee, if thou wilt fall down and worship me.

10.) Then saith Jesus unto him, Get thee hence, Satan: for it is written, Thou shalt worship the Lord thy God, and him only shalt thou serve.

MATTHEW 4:1-10

My dear Christian friend, Satan tempted Jesus in the areas that he thought Jesus was week. First, he tempted HIM with food, because Jesus had just fasted, then he tried to get Jesus to kill Himself, then he tried to get Jesus to worship him by offering HIM the world.

But Praise GOD, Jesus exercised great temperance every time HE was tempted. It is essential that you realize how Jesus exercised that great temperance, because you will need to follow HIS example and do the very same thing HE did. Notice that Jesus responded to every temptation with the Word of GOD. HE would say it is written and quote a verse from the Word of GOD. You are going to need to know the Word of GOD for yourself, so that when Satan tempts you to get out of control or fall weak to his tricks, you will know how to exercise temperance like Jesus did.

My dear Christian friend, GOD wants to give you total restoration in temperance, and the time for you to allow HIM to do it is now.

GOD wants to give you total restoration in temperance, so you will be strong in every area of your life.

GOD wants to give you total restoration in temperance, so that you will be able to overcome Satan and his unclean army when they come to tempt you in the areas they think you are weak.

GOD wants to give you total restoration in temperance, so you will be mighty in GOD'S ways, and in all you do.

Praise the LORD! GOD wants to give you total restoration in temperance, and the time for you to allow HIM to do it is now.

Then you will be able to live that abundant, victorious life that Jesus wants you to live, and enjoy the Bible's full rewards.

That, my friend, is "Total Restoration."

GOD is good!

Chapter Eleven

Total Restoration with God

17.) Therefore, if any man be in Christ, he is a new Creature: old things are passed away; behold all things are become new.

18.) And all things are of God, who hath reconciled us to himself by Jesus Christ, and hath given to us the ministry of reconciliation;

19.) To wit, That God was in Christ, reconciling the world unto himself, not imputing their trespasses unto them; and hath committed unto us the word of reconciliation.

20.) Now then we are ambassadors for Christ, as though God did beseech you by us: we pray you in Christ's stead, be ye reconciled to God.

2nd CORINTHIANS 5:17-20

My dear Christian friend, according to this passage, GOD hath reconciled us to Himself through Jesus Christ. Therefore, when we accept Jesus Christ's work of reconciling us back to GOD, we are accepting total restoration with GOD.

GOD wants to give us total restoration with HIM, and the time for us to allow HIM to do it is now.

If we will allow HIM to, GOD will give us total restoration with HIM, and everything we need will be imparted to us by HIM. Praise the LORD, if we will accept total restoration with GOD, we will eventually have total restoration in every area of our lives.

Praise GOD! I have already showed you that GOD wants to give you total restoration in love, joy, peace, longsuffering, gentleness, goodness, faith, meekness and temperance. But I want to tell you now that there is so much more GOD is offering us, if we will receive it, and allow HIM to work in our lives.

My dear Christian friend, GOD also wants to give us total restoration in prosperity. HE wants to bless us abundantly, and HE wants us to prosper in every area of our lives.

Let's look at a verse to prove this.

Let them shout for joy, and be glad, that favour my righteous cause: yea, let them say continually, let the Lord be magnified, which hath pleasure in the prosperity of his Servant.

PSALMS 35:27

Praise the LORD! See right there it says, the LORD takes pleasure in the prosperity of HIS Servant.

My dear Christian friend, GOD wants to give you total restoration in prosperity, and the time for you to allow HIM to do it is now.

When you allow GOD to give you total restoration in prosperity, HE will supply your every need.

Let's look at a verse to prove this.

But my God shall supply all your needs according to his riches in glory by Christ Jesus.

PHILIPPIANS 4:19

This is good news my friend. GOD wants to give you total restoration in prosperity, and HE wants to supply all of your needs. Praise GOD!

GOD wants you to prosper in HIM in every area of your life.

My dear Christian friend, GOD also wants to give you total restoration in your health. GOD wants to heal you, and make your whole body healthy. Actually, HE wants you healthy so you can do HIS Will, and what HE wants you to do for HIM. Believe me, GOD has plenty of things you can do for HIM if you are healthy enough. GOD wants to give you total restoration in health.

Let's look at a verse to prove this.

For I will restore health unto thee, and I will heal thee of thy wounds, saith the Lord; because they called thee an outcast, saying, This is Zion whom no man seeketh after.

JEREMIAH 30:17

In the very first line of this verse, GOD said HE would restore health unto us. This is a promise. If GOD will do it for one, HE will do it for all. GOD wants to give you total restoration in your health, so you can go into the world and tell people about HIM.

Praise the LORD! GOD wants to give you total restoration in health, and the time for you to allow HIM to do it is now.

GOD wants you to prosper and be in good health.

Let's look at a verse to prove this.

Beloved, I wish above all things that thou mayest Prosper and be in health, even as thy soul Prospereth.

3rd JOHN 1:2

Glory to GOD! Here is another verse saying that GOD wants us to prosper and be in good health.

GOD wants to give you total restoration in prosperity and health, and the time for you to allow HIM to do it is now. GOD is a good GOD, and HE wants to give you total restoration in every area of your life, and the time for you to allow HIM to do it is now.

Dear friend, Satan and his unclean army does not want you to have total restoration with GOD. Believe me, he will do everything he can to stop you from serving GOD. But always remember the battle is not flesh and blood, it's not people trying to stop you from serving GOD, it is unclean Spirits working through people. Please remember that. I assure you that if you are trying to love people the way GOD wants you to, someone will come across your path that almost seems unlovable, but if you will just continue to show them the love of GOD, you will always overcome. Satan and his unclean army don't want you to have it, but GOD wants to give you total restoration in every area of your life, and the time for you to allow HIM to do it is now.

My dear Christian friend, another thing GOD wants to give you total restoration in is righteousness. HE wants you to share in HIS Righteousness, and the only way to do it is by being in Christ.

Let's look at a couple of verses to prove this.

20.) Now then we are ambassadors for Christ, as though God did beseech you by us: we Pray you in Christ's stead, be ye reconciled to God.

21.) For he hath made him to be sin for us, who knew no sin; that we might be made the righteousness of God in him.

2nd CORINTHIANS 5:20-21

My dear friend, the first verse says, be ye reconciled to God. In other words, accept total restoration with GOD. The second verse says that Christ was made sin for us, that we might be made the righteousness of GOD in HIM.

See, Jesus Christ knew no sin, and HE made a way for us to share in HIS very own righteousness. Look at the last two words in verse 21, it says, "in Him." That is in Christ, we can be made the righteousness of GOD.

Praise the LORD! Now that is true righteousness. My dear friend, GOD does indeed want to give you total restoration in righteousness, and the time for you to allow HIM to do it is now.

My dear Christian friend, GOD wants to give us all a Crown of Righteousness. HE wants us to share in HIS Righteousness here and now, and then when we pass on from this world, or if Christ returns before then, GOD wants to give all of us a Crown of Righteousness.

Let's look at a verse to prove this.

Henceforth there is laid up for me a Crown of righteousness, which the Lord, the righteous judge, shall give me at that day: and not to me only, but unto all them also that love his appearing.

2nd TIMOTHY 4:8

My dear friend, according to this verse, GOD wants to give all of us a Crown of Righteousness. Praise the LORD! GOD wants to give us total restoration in HIS Righteousness, then HE wants to give us a Crown of Righteousness. GOD is good!

My dear Christian friend, let me warn you that Satan and his unclean army will do everything they can to keep you from walking in GOD'S Righteousness, and from you getting your Crown of Righteousness. The devil will tempt you in every way he can to get you to live an unrighteous life. But if you will just trust in GOD, HE will give you the strength to overcome Satan and his unclean army. Like I said, GOD is good, and HE wants the very best for you. Praise the LORD! GOD wants to give you total restoration in righteousness, and the time for you to allow HIM to do it is now.

Dear friend, GOD does indeed want to give you total restoration with HIM, and HE wants to give you total restoration in every area of your life.

GOD wants to give you total restoration in every area of your life, so you can live an abundant, victorious life in every area of your life.

Jesus said in the Bible, that Satan will try to steal from us, kill us, and destroy us in every area of our life. But Glory to GOD, Jesus said that HE came so we could have an abundant, victorious life.

Let's look at a verse to prove this.

The thief cometh not, but for to steal, and to kill, and to destroy: I am come that they might have life, and that they might have it more abundantly.

JOHN 10:10

Praise the LORD! Jesus told us right here in this verse, that the thief, (Satan) will be out to steal, kill and destroy us. But Glory to GOD, Jesus said that HE came to give us a life, and even more abundantly. That means that if we will allow HIM to, GOD will give us total restoration in every area of our lives.

When you allow GOD to give you total restoration with HIM, and total restoration in every area of your life, you will be able to overcome Satan and his unclean army, no matter what storm or temptation they may tempt you with.

In Christ, you can be more than a Conqueror.

Let's look at a verse to prove this.

Nay, in all these things we are more than Conquerors through him that loved us.

ROMANS 8:37

Glory to GOD! This verse says in all these things, that means whatever Satan and his unclean army may bring your way, we are more than Conquerors through HIM who loved us, (Jesus).

When Satan and his unclean army try to steal your love, joy, peace, longsuffering, gentleness, goodness, faith, meekness, prosperity, health, righteousness, or anything else GOD says you can have, just call on Jesus, and in HIM you will come out being more than a Conqueror.

My dear Christian friend, GOD does indeed want you to have total restoration in HIM, and total restoration in every area of your life.

If GOD says you can have total restoration in love, you can have it. If GOD says you can have total restoration in joy, you can have it. If GOD says you can have total restoration in peace, you can have it. If GOD says you can have total restoration in longsuffering, you can have it. If GOD says you can have total restoration in gentleness, you can have it. If GOD says you can have total restoration in faith, you can have it. If GOD says you can have total restoration in meekness, you can have it. If GOD says you can have total restoration in temperance, you can have it. If GOD says you can have total restoration in prosperity, you can have it. If GOD says you can have total restoration in health, you can have it. If GOD says you can have total restoration in righteousness, you can have it. If GOD says you can have total restoration in every area of your life, you can have it, and no one can take it from you.

My dear Christian friend, GOD wants to give you total restoration with HIM, and total restoration in every area of your life, and the time for you to allow HIM to do it is now.

So dear friend, I encourage you today to allow GOD to give you total restoration with HIM, and total restoration in every area of your life. It is what GOD wants, and what is best for you.

So, I say to you, please, receive total restoration today.

Then you will be able to live that abundant, victorious life that Jesus wants you to live, and enjoy the Bible's full rewards.

That my friend, is "Total Restoration."

Hallelujah!

Power Prayer

For Salvation and to be baptized in the Holy Spirit.

Father GOD, I come to you as humbly as I know how. LORD, your Word says in 1st JOHN 1:9, "If we confess our sins, he is faithful and just to forgive us our sins, and to cleanse us from all unrighteousness." So, I confess to you that I have sinned in many ways. I now repent and turn away from my sins, and I ask you to forgive me and cleanse me from all of my unrighteousness, in the name of Jesus.

Father, your Word also says in ROMANS 10:9-10, "that if thou shalt confess with thy mouth the Lord Jesus, and shalt believe in thine heart that God raised him from the dead, thou shalt be saved. For with the heart man believeth unto righteousness; and with the mouth confession is made unto Salvation."

So, I confess with my mouth that I believe Jesus died on the Cross so I can be saved, and I believe with all my heart that GOD raised HIM from the dead, and I ask you to come into my life and save me. I now accept Jesus as my LORD and Savior, and I believe with all my heart that your Word is true, and that I am saved by grace!

Father, your Word also says in the Book of LUKE 11:13, "If ye then being evil, know how to give good gifts unto your children: how much more shall your Heavenly Father give the Holy Spirit to them that ask Him?"

So, Father, I ask you to give me the gift of the Holy Spirit. I ask you to fill me till my cup runs over, and allow me to successfully function in the gifts of the Spirit that are mentioned in your Word. So that I will become an effective witness for Jesus, and a blessing to others for the rest of my life. In Jesus' name I pray, Amen.

If you have prayed this prayer, you can believe without a doubt that you are saved. The Bible says, "you shall be saved." That is a promise, and it is also a promise that GOD will fill you with the Holy Spirit if you ask HIM.

So now you need to join a good Church, and sincerely turn away from your old sinful life, and walk in and enjoy the new Spirit filled life that GOD has given you. The old you should start fading into the past, and the new you will start shining brightly as you seek to serve GOD in all you do.

About the author

Thomas Couch has a GED, and some College credits (no degree) with MERCER, and BREWTON PARKER Universities. He was an Honor Roll Student while he attended college.

The name of his ministry is "REVIVE-ALL Ministries." This Ministry is an outreach of "Souls Harbor Word of Faith Church" in Canton, Georgia where he was ordained and licensed to minister as a Preacher of the Gospel. He has a Certificate for "Caring for People God's Way" with Light University, that is approved by the American Association of Christian Counselors Board.

He is currently a member of "Colorful Crow Writers Community," and he is engaged in a writing ministry.

GOD gave Thomas this material to write in efforts to minister to GOD'S People, to reach the lost, and to abundantly bless all who will enjoy its contents.

He says it is proof that with GOD you can do all things through Christ who strengthens you. (PHILIPPIANS 4:13)

He prays it will be a blessing to everyone that it reaches.